COASTAL
HABITATS

BY
BARBARA TAYLOR

WHERE LAND MEETS THE SEA

HERMIT AT HOME

Hermit crabs look clumsy as they crawl over the shore looking for dead animal remains. Yet they are well suited for shoreline survival. The large front pincer can be held across the opening of its shell, sealing the entrance shut. Then the crab can be rolled about by the waves without damage to its body inside the shell. The crab's body also remains moist inside the shell when the tide goes out.

From rough, rocky shores and hot sandy beaches, to muddy estuaries and mangrove forests – coastlines are fascinating meeting places between the land and the sea. Most shoreline plants and animals live in the sea, but have adapted to living out of water for part of the day. A few, however, are only land dwellers. These include insects high on the shore, plants on sand dunes and birds that nest on cliffs. The twice-daily ebb and flow of the tide exposes coastline creatures to huge changes in temperature and water levels. These changes are as great as seasonal changes on land, such as summer turning to winter. But on the coast these changes take place every day instead of every year, making it a very challenging habitat for wildlife.

BEACH BURROWERS

A sandy beach often seems to be empty of life but most of its inhabitants are buried underneath the surface. These range from microscopic bacteria to all sorts of shellfish, crustaceans (such as crabs), worms and sea urchins. They trap tiny food particles from the water, brought in by the tides or filter nutrients from the sand – rather like an earthworm eats soil.

FOSSIL FINDS

Fossils found in rocks on beaches help to find out the age of the rocks or how much the sea is rising. Fossils of ocean creatures, such as this ammonite, show that the rocks were once under the sea. Ammonites were shellfish related to modern-day octopuses, squid and nautiluses. When the animal was alive, a head with tentacles stuck out of the end of the shell, but it could scurry back inside and close the opening. Ammonites lived hundreds of millions of years ago.

HIDING PLACES

A rocky shore has a number of places for animals to feed and shelter. They can hide under rocks and boulders, among tangled seaweed or in rock pools. Some creatures, such as piddocks and sea urchins, even drill themselves into the solid rock. Shoreline rocks can be dangerous for passing ships but lighthouses warn them to stay well clear of dangerous waters at night.

CONE PROTECTOR

Limpets are expert at clinging to rocks with their muscular feet. The cone shape of the limpet's shell gives it a wide base for clinging to rocks without being washed away by the water. Waves and tides crash over the limpets without dislodging them. Limpets usually move about when the tide is in, feeding on algae on the rocks. They return to their home base when the tide goes out.

CLIFF COLONIES

Many seabirds nest on rocky cliffs where it is difficult for predators to reach their eggs, but where they are still close to their food supply in the sea. Puffins live in nest burrows on cliff tops. The large, colourful bill of the Atlantic puffin plays an important role in courtship. Outside of the breeding season, the puffin's bill becomes smaller and less brightly coloured.

LIFE BETWEEN THE TIDES

T he lives and activities of shore creatures are controlled largely by the tides, which creep up the shore and then down again, roughly twice every 24 hours. In some parts of the world, such as the Mediterranean, the tides are very small, but in other places the tides go out as much as 3 km (2 miles). Creatures living between the tides have to survive in two environments, both in and out of the water. Creatures that can survive out of the water for long periods, live high up the shore. Those that can only handle short periods out of the water live on the lower shore, near the sea. There are often different zones of life, stretching from the sea to the top of the shore. At low tide, shore creatures are exposed to drying winds, the Sun's ultraviolet rays, high and low temperatures and attacks from land-based predators.

SURFING SNAIL

The South African plough snail has mastered a way of moving with the tides. As the waves moves up the shore, the plough snail emerges from its hiding place in the sand and sucks water into its foot. This makes a sort of surfboard on which the snail surfs up the beach. At the high-water mark, where the waves leave all sorts of dead and decaying food, the snail feeds on stranded sea creatures. As the tide retreats, the plough snail surfs back down the beach.

Barnacles out of water

HEAD STANDS

Barnacles float in the water for a while before settling down on the rocks. They are attracted by the smell of existing barnacle colonies and tend to settle near them. Experts say that a barnacle 'welds its head to the rock and spends its life kicking food into its mouth with its legs'. When the tide is out, the barnacle pulls its legs back inside its shell and seals the opening.

A barnacle under water

WHY TIDES HAPPEN

THE MOON'S ORBIT

THE EARTH

The tides are caused mainly by the pull of the Moon's gravity on the Earth's oceans. As the Moon orbits the Earth, the oceans are pulled towards it, making high tides on that side of the Earth – and on the opposite side because of the Earth's spin. The Sun's gravity also pulls the oceans but its effect is much weaker because it is much farther away. Twice a month, when the Sun, Moon and Earth are in a line, the pull of the Moon and Sun combine to produce extra high and low tides, called spring tides. When the Sun, Moon and Earth form a right angle, the Sun's pull works against the Moon's pull, making less extreme tides, called neap tides.

BURROWING SHELL

Cockles live on sandy shores, burrowing into the sand with their foot. They only burrow deep enough to cover the shell and sometimes roll over the sand to change their feeding area. The shell probably helps to hold the animal in the sand. When the tide is in, cockles filter tiny food particles, such as plankton, from the water. Cockles survive best in mid to low shore levels where the tide flows rapidly in and out. Over 10,000 cockles can live in just 1 sq metre (10 sq ft).

BEACH STAR

Starfish usually live below the level of low tide, or in rock pools. If they are washed up on a beach, they will dry out and die. To avoid this happening, starfish have hundreds of tube-feet to cling tightly to rocks, sand and other surfaces. They are also protected by an external skeleton of tough plates. If a starfish's arm is crushed by a boulder, or bitten off by a predator, it can grow a new arm.

COASTLINES OF THE WORLD

Coastlines are very special and different places. They range from the sun-baked tropical shores of Australia and Indonesia to the temperate shorelines of Europe and the frozen coasts of Arctic Canada. Some, such as the shores of the Galapagos Islands, are home to wildlife that is found nowhere else in the world. Coastlines change according to the climate in different parts of the world. Coral reefs, for instance, grow only in warm, clean waters in the tropics. Mangrove trees are also found along tropical shores and are adapted to grow in seashore mud. In cooler parts of the world, such as Northern Europe and North America, sandy, rocky and muddy shores are less exotic, but still full of creatures with amazing adaptations. The muddy shores of European estuaries are particularly important as feeding and resting places for migrating birds. Polar shores come alive in summer, as feeding and nesting areas for whales, seals and millions of seabirds.

EUROPEAN SHORE

Life on northern European shores is very exposed to the Sun, the wind and the waves. Yet rocks and seaweeds provide shelter for a large number of creatures and a little way beneath the sand a host of creatures survive in a relatively constant environment.

However, the weather does change with the seasons and winter storms may pound these coasts with amazing force, removing old or poorly attached individuals.

CORAL COASTS

For hundreds of millions of years, coral reefs have grown along tropical shores where the sea temperatures are always above 18°C (64°F). They grow only in shallow water up to 70 metres (230 ft) deep, because the algae that live in the coral need sunlight to make their food. The reef itself is made of the skeletons of coral animals and the living coral on top. In ideal conditions, coral reefs grow up to 25 mm (1 inch) a year.

ORCA COAST

These dorsal fins belong to killer whales, or orcas, living off the coast of British Columbia, Canada. These whales will chase fish and other prey into quite shallow waters. Killer whales live in oceans all over the world, but are most common in cooler climates. They are a top predator around polar coasts. Whales of all kinds breed near tropical coasts but migrate to polar areas to feed there in summer.

MANGROVE COASTS

Mangrove, or tidal forest, grows on river estuaries and sheltered muddy inlets in the tropics. Forming a barrier between the land and the sea, the mangrove roots protects the muddy coasts from flooding or being washed away by the waves and the tides. A large number of animals, such as fish and crabs, live in the shelter of the trees.

GALAPAGOS COASTS

From sea lions and marine iguanas to cormorants and frigate birds, the coasts of the Galapagos Islands teem with unique wildlife. Sea lions breed on the islands in the Pacific Ocean about 1,000 km (620 miles) west of South America. Warm waters from the Pacific and cool waters from the Antarctic both flow past the Galapagos. This means that animals from cold places, such as penguins, live side by side with tropical species, such as flamingos.

ROCKY SHORES

The most obvious plants on rocky shores are the red, green and brown seaweeds. They have thick outer layers and a small surface area to help stop water loss when they are exposed to the air. Most successful animals of the high shore have shells, which may be white to reflect heat in warmer climates. Shellfish stop water loss at low tide by keeping their shells tightly closed or by clamping them firmly to the rocks. They may also be able to breathe air as well as take in oxygen from the water. Animals that cannot stand being exposed to the air, such as sea anemones, worms and sponges, have to shelter among rocks or in tide pools as the tide goes out.

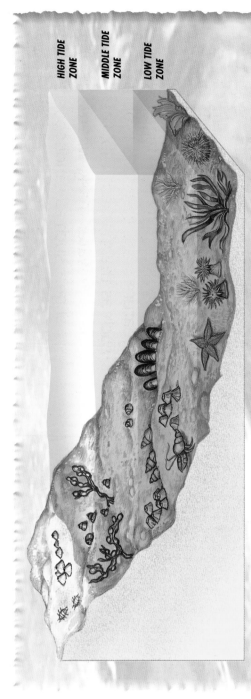

HIGH TIDE ZONE

MIDDLE TIDE ZONE

LOW TIDE ZONE

ZONES OF LIFE

Plants and animals live in zones on all intertidal beaches, but the zones are most obvious on rocky shores. There are three major zones: the low tide zone, with animals such as starfish and sea squirts, and seaweeds such as kelps; the middle tide zone, with animals such as barnacles and mussels, and seaweeds such as wracks; and the high tide zone, with animals such as periwinkles and limpets, as well as lichens. Plants and animals are restricted to a zone according to how long they can survive out of the water.

MUSSEL ROPES

Mussels anchor themselves to rocks or even other mussels, using strong, sticky threads, which work like the guy ropes on a tent. The mussels produce the threads as a thick fluid, which hardens in the seawater. Mussels depend on the waves and tides to bring their food. They open their shells slightly under the water, and filter microscopic food particles from the water.

SEALED SHELL

On the back of this common whelk's foot is a special plate that seals the opening of the shell when the whelk retreats inside. The shell is also thick and ridged to help the whelk survive the pounding of the waves. Whelks lay their eggs in a spongy ball, which may be washed up high on the beach.

SANDY SHORES

Sandy beaches have fewer creatures than rocky shores, although some animals, such as worms and bivalve molluscs, may exist in large numbers. Buried beneath the sand are thousands of wriggling bodies. As many as 8,000 burrowing clams have been counted in only 1 sq metre (10 sq ft). A few centimetres below the sand, conditions are much the same whether the tide is in or out, or whether it is warm or cold, sunny or raining. A thin film of water surrounds each grain of sand, sticking them together so that the sand is always moist. Burrowing creatures feed on debris brought in by the tide, but there are also predators, such as the masked crab, the burrowing starfish and seashore birds. At the high water mark, where bits of seaweed, shells and other debris collect, scavengers such as sandhoppers and turnstones find plenty to eat.

CUNNING GULLS

Gulls sometimes paddle their feet up and down on the surface of the sand to bring cockles and other hidden animals to the surface. They may also carry shellfish away to a hard surface and drop them so they smash open. Gulls are real scavengers and their strong beaks can usually deal with most kinds of food. They can even crack open the shells of crabs to get at the juicy meat inside.

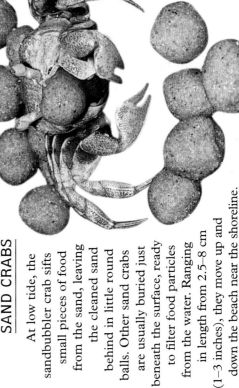

SAND CRABS

At low tide, the sandbubbler crab sifts small pieces of food from the sand, leaving the cleaned sand behind in little round balls. Other sand crabs are usually buried just beneath the surface, ready to filter food particles from the water. Ranging in length from 2.5–8 cm (1–3 inches), they move up and down the beach near the shoreline.

BURROWING ANIMALS

At low tide, there is often signs of life beneath the surface. Squiggly mounds of sand, rather like piles of spaghetti, are the waste sand squirted out the end of a lugworm's burrow (right) when it has finished feeding. The grainy feeding tubes of the sand mason worm may also be sticking out of the sand. The worm makes this protective tube from sticky mucus to which grains of sand become attached.

SAND DUNE SECRETS

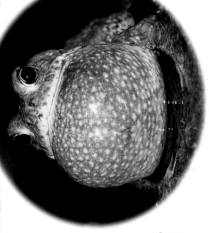

S and dunes sometimes build up along a shore where wind-blown sand is held in place by plants such as marram grass. The dry sand of the dunes contains little organic material and the surface may become very hot on a sunny day. Yet some creatures still live here. Wolf spiders survive by hunting flies blown into the dunes. The spiders are eaten by the rare sand lizard. Rabbits find it easy to burrow in the dunes and there are plenty of plants for them to eat. Shelducks may use old rabbit burrows as nesting sites. Other birds, such as skylarks, terns, gulls and plovers also nest on the dunes, although foxes may raid their nests. Sheltered damp hollows between the larger dunes, known as 'slacks', contain orchids, rushes and other marsh plants. The dune slacks are the breeding grounds of frogs and toads.

TERRIFYING TOAD

The rare natterjack toad lives in dune slacks. It puffs out its vocal sac to make a loud call, which usually begins just before sunset. On still, quiet evenings, a chorus of several toads can be heard over 2 km (1¼ miles) or more. When it is disturbed or alarmed, this toad inflates its body, raises its rump and produces a horrible smelling secretion from its skin.

LAZY LIZARD

Sand lizards are cold-blooded so their bodies are always at the same temperature as their surroundings. They need the warmth of the Sun to keep their bodies working. Sand lizards lay their eggs in the sand, using the warmth of the sand to help the development of their eggs.

MIGHTY MARRAM

Marram grass has tough leaves rolled into tubes that collect valuable moisture. It can put out roots from its stem, so it climbs 'step-by-step' up the growing dunes, holding the sand together as it goes. Its roots push down into the sand to reach fresh water in the cold sand deep below. When a shoot is buried by the sand, it produces a bud that pushes up another shoot. In one year, marram grass can spread up to 9 metres (29 ft) sideways and 1 metre (3 ft) vertically, helping the dunes to grow in the process.

DUNE PLANTS

Dune plants have several features that help them survive the winds, the heat, the lack of moisture and salt, blown from the sea. Sea holly (right) and sea bindweed have stiff 'varnished' leaves to stop water escaping and give protection against sand blown by the wind. Hairy plants trap dew on their stalks and leaves. Many plants grow along the ground to keep out of the wind. Others have huge root systems to hold them in place securely and reach water underground.

POISONOUS MOTHS

Day-flying cinnabar moths feed from dune flowers and their striped caterpillars (right) are often seen feeding on plants such as ragwort or groundsel. The red warning colours of the moth and the caterpillar warn of their poisonous bodies and protect them from predators such as lizards, birds and mammals. The poisons come from the caterpillars' food plants and are passed on to the adult moth.

LIFE IN A ROCK POOL

Rock pools on the shore are full of a variety of plant and animal life. The shallow pools have fewer plants and animals but deeper ones are very busy. Rock pools provide permanently wet refuges at all levels on the shore. Yet it is tough to survive in the environment of a rock pool. Its inhabitants have to cope with great changes in temperature, but changes in the level of oxygen and carbon dioxide are often most dramatic. At night, when the plants are not photosynthesising (or making food), carbon dioxide builds up but oxygen levels fall as both plants and animals carry on using up oxygen. Extra carbon dioxide at night makes the water more acidic. The reverse happens during the day as plants use up carbon dioxide and give off oxygen. There is a constant movement of life between the rock pools as animals search for food or seek to avoid predators.

SEAWEED SURVIVAL

The brown seaweed called bladder wrack has flat fronds with air-filled sacs. The sacs help the seaweed float when the tide is in, and keeps its branches held apart for photosynthesis. Special slime covers the seaweed and protects it from drying out at low tide. The seaweed is firmly attached to the rocks by a long, flexible stalk and a holdfast, to clasp it into place. The orange branches contain the spores that will grow into new seaweeds.

JELLY FLOWERS

Sea anemones survive well in rock pools because they are usually underwater and can feed all day. They may look like flowers but they are hollow, jelly-like animals related to jellyfish and corals. Their colourful tentacles spell danger for small sea creatures, such as shrimps, which are stung by the tentacles and pulled in towards the mouth. To protect themselves from danger, or drying out, most anemones can pull in their tentacles and become jelly-like blobs.

POOL PRAWNS

Most rock pools have a large shrimp and prawn population but they are almost transparent, so are not easy to see. The chameleon prawn can change colour to match its surroundings, although it takes about a week to do so. Prawns can also shoot backwards suddenly to avoid danger. They can live in a wide range of temperatures, but move to warm, open ocean waters at the beginning of winter.

STAR TURN

The common starfish has a very special way of eating mussels. First it wraps its arms around the shell and pulls hard until the exhausted mussel allows the two halves of its shell to open a little. Then the starfish turns its stomach inside out and slips it down inside the mussel to slowly eat the contents.

ROCK POOL FISH

Rock pool fish, such as blennies (right) and gobies, are usually well camouflaged and shaped so that they can easily wriggle in among rocks and seaweed. Their eyes are often near the top of their heads to watch for predators from above. Lumpsuckers and clingfish have suckers to hang on to rocks when waves crash over them or the tide goes out, taking the water from the pools. In spring, shore fish come to rock pools to breed. The young move to warmer offshore waters for the winter.

ROCK POOL LIFE

This rock pool in South Africa has an large amount of life – creatures and plants all crammed together in their wet home.

The empty shell, or test, of a sea urchin. The white knobs show where the spines were attached.

Starfish crawl into rock pools to find damp places to shelter in low tide.

The conical shape of the limpet's shell helps it resist the pounding of the waves.

Crabs hide in rock pools to stop their bodies from drying out. They sort through the debris for food particles.

At high tide, sea urchins feed on tiny plants by scraping rocks with their powerful teeth.

Sea lettuce is green seaweed that looks like the lettuce we eat in salads.

GANNET LIFTS

Gannets and other seabirds fly on currents of air that rise up over the cliffs. Gannets are strong fliers but the currents help them save their energy. The gannets have to make many trips to and from the nesting sites to bring food to their young. Gannets use their strong pointed bills to catch fish and also to attack other gannets that come close to their nesting space. They build large nests of seaweed, feathers, grass and soil.

PLASTER NEST

Kittiwakes attach their cup-shaped nests to the rock face with mud and droppings. They can nest on ledges that are too narrow even for guillemots. It is usual to see only two or three young in the nest until they fly at about six weeks old. Kittiwakes are named after the sound of their call.

EGG ROLL

Guillemots do not make nests. Their eggs are pear shaped and if they are blown by the wind they spin round rather than fall off the cliff. Each guillemot has a different pattern on its egg to help it to recognise which ones are its own. Some have red stripes, others have chocolate blotches and some have green and black squiggles all over them.

LIFE ON A LEDGE

The sight of hundreds of seabirds swooping and screeching around a cliff nesting site is incredible. The birds nest at different levels to share the space (below right). Near the top of the cliffs nest gannets, gulls and puffins, with guillemots, razorbills and kittiwakes in the middle, and larger cormorants and shags at the bottom. The cliffs are high and steep, so keep the eggs and chicks safe from most predators. Also the young birds are close to the sea when they are ready to leave the nest. Cliff plants cannot follow the birds to warmer climates when the summer breeding season is over. Instead, they must put up with the constant salty spray, rain, frost, snow and landslides. Long roots help them to hold on to thin cracks in the rock, and their fleshy leaves and waxy surfaces reduce water loss.

GROUND FLOOR

Shags and cormorants nest at the bottom of cliffs, building nests of sticks and seaweed, lined with grass. Shags defend their nests fiercely. They refuse to leave during an attack and thrust their beaks forward at enemies. After swimming, shags and cormorants often stand with their wings open to let their feathers dry in the breeze.

VEGGY CLIFFS

The relatives of well-known vegetables grow on cliffs, such as sea carrot (left), sea cabbage and sea beet. Sea beet is quick to grow in new broken ground so likes the unstable cliff environment, where pieces of cliff often break off and slide down into the sea. In the breeding season, birds kill the plants by trampling on them and covering them with their droppings. But small amounts of droppings provide nutrients for some plants such as sea campion. Tree mallow grows well among a jumble of herring gull and cormorant nests.

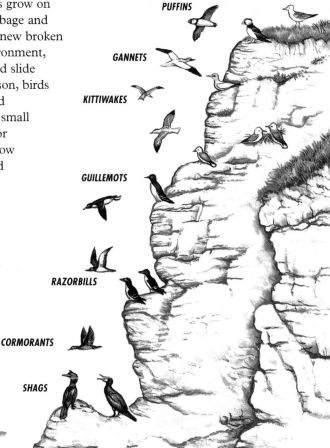

GULLS

PUFFINS

GANNETS

KITTIWAKES

GUILLEMOTS

RAZORBILLS

CORMORANTS

SHAGS

WHERE RIVERS MEET THE SEA

SHARING FOOD

A variety of wading birds can feed together because their bills are different lengths and shapes, so they can feed at different depths in the mud. Short-billed plovers feed on spire shells at the surface. Knot and redshank, with bills twice as long, probe into the top layer of mud for shrimps and small worms. Curlews (above) and godwits, with the longest bills of all, probe down deep enough to reach the lugworms and drag them out of their burrows.

When the freshwater of rivers slows down and flows into the salty water of the sea, the mud and silt it carries drifts to the bottom. Over hundreds of years, the mud builds up, plants grow, and a saltmarsh forms. The main problem with living in these muddy estuaries is the huge changes in the saltwater caused by the tides, and the amount of river water – which depends on how much rain has fallen. If a sea creature, with blood as salty as seawater, is placed in freshwater, it will absorb water, swell up and die. Twice a day, most of the mud will be exposed to the air and there are also dramatic changes between summer and winter. Estuary inhabitants must be able to withstand a great changes but a few creatures, such as worms and shellfish, survive in large numbers. A quarter of a million sludge worms can live in just 1 sq metre (10 sq ft). Estuary mud is a rich source of nutrients, from both sea and land.

WATER CONSERVATION

A plant called the glasswort begins the process of turning mudflats into a saltmarsh. It looks rather like a desert plant because its stems also store water and its leathery leaves and stems prevent water loss. Glasswort needs to keep a lot of water because it cannot take in freshwater from the sea and the very salty seawater tends to dry up its freshwater. Long ago, people collected glasswort and burned it, because its ashes can be used to make glass.

MUD TO MARSH

Glasswort traps mud, which raises the level of the sea bottom and allows grasses, rushes and other plants, such as sea aster (left) and sea lavender, to grow. Plant debris becomes tangled among the stems, which traps more mud. The level of the saltmarsh gradually rises until only the highest tides flood it. Only a few ducks and geese graze on the tough and salty plants. Wading birds and ducks nest among the vegetation in summer.

PINCER POWER

Ragworms are active predators, seizing prey in their jaws. They live in slimy burrows in the mud, reaching out to eat plant and animal remains and catch creatures such as shrimps as they pass by. Ragworms are omnivores and feed on almost anything they can find. On each body segment are a pair of flat, paddle-like legs. The ragworm uses these for crawling, swimming and breathing. Stiff bristles on the legs help the ragworm to grip surfaces.

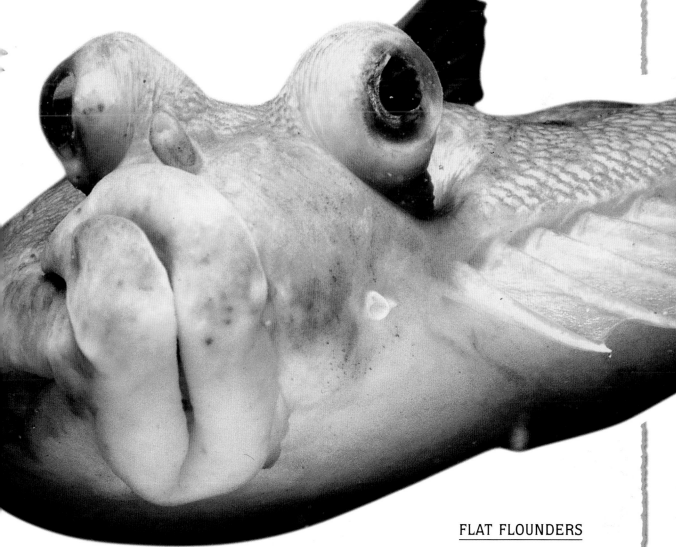

FLAT FLOUNDERS

The flounder is a typical estuary fish. It spawns in the sea, but the adults can survive in an estuary or even in freshwater for a long time. Rivers are an important nursery ground for the flounder. They live on the bottom and feed on invertebrates, such as marine worms, small crustaceans and shellfish. Since they lie on their sides, flounders have both eyes on the side of their heads.

MANGROVE SWAMPS

A round 240,000 sq km (93,000 sq miles) of sheltered shores in the tropics have mangrove swamps along their borders. Mangroves are trees adapted to live in wet, salty, muddy places. They have spreading roots to hold them in the slushy, smelly mud. Some of them 'breathe' through small roots that stick up through the mud. Breathing roots are vital because there is very little oxygen in the wet mud. The high tide covers the base of the trees and a wide variety of animals live in the mud, on the mangrove roots and in the branches. The warm shallow waters are an ideal home for young fish, which are hunted by crocodiles, alligators, snakes and birds, such as storks, ibises and herons. Crabs live in the mud and scuttle about in the jungle of roots at low tide, scavenging for food that is brought in by the tide.

MARVELLOUS MANGROVES

Red mangroves keep themselves in place with a tangle of stilt or prop roots. Mud slowly collects around the roots and builds up into soil. So the mangrove trees help to extend the coasts farther out to sea. Their special, torpedo-shaped seeds germinate while still hanging on the tree. When they fall off, some stick into the mud and sprout into new trees. Others are carried out to sea by the tides and may drift hundreds of kilometres before growing on another salty patch of coastal mud.

FISH OUT OF WATER

Mudskippers are finger-sized fish that often spend more time out of water than in. They move across the mud in a series of 'skips' by wriggling their tails. They can even climb onto mangrove roots using their stumpy fins. When the tide is out, or when danger threatens, they burrow into the mud. Some mudskippers claim territory, building low mud ridges along the borders to keep neighbours out. The mud walls also stop the seawater from draining away at low tide.

CLIMBING SNAILS

Sea snails feed on algae on the surface of the mud at low tide but climb up the mangrove roots before the tide washes seawater over them. This helps them to escape from fish that might eat them. Every month, the tides rise so high that the snails would not have enough time to get out of harm's way. So they climb even higher, rather than crawling down.

WATER PISTOL

One of the fish seen around the mangrove roots at high tide is the archerfish. It spits a stream of water up into the air – like a water pistol – to knock insects into the water, where it immediately gobbles them up.

LOUDSPEAKER NOSE

Male proboscis monkeys have a large nose, which acts as a loudspeaker for the male's honking calls. These warn other proboscis monkeys of danger. Proboscis monkeys are very skilled at living in the trees, leaping through the mangrove forests using their long tails to balance. If danger threatens, they will dive and swim under the water. Proboscis monkeys live only in the mangrove forests on the island of Borneo. They spend most of their lives high up in the mangroves, feeding on leaves and some fruits and flowers.

HOW REEFS FORM

Coral reefs sometimes grow around the shores of tropical islands. If sea levels rise, or the island sinks, the coral continues to grow upwards, forming a ring of coral separated from the island by a stretch of water. If the island disappears beneath the surface of the sea, a ring of coral, called an atoll, is left behind. The lagoon in the middle of the atoll is shallow, but the seaward side of the atoll is surrounded by deep water.

FRINGING REEF

A volcano grows from the ocean bed. Corals grow around its slopes.

BARRIER REEF

The volcano collapses and begins to sink.

ATOLL **LAGOON**

The volcano vanishes, leaving behind an atoll.

HELPFUL SHRIMP

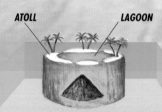

Some reef shrimps set up 'cleaning stations' in places where they are visited by a number of fish. The shrimps nibble at the mucus covering the fish's scales and may also remove any external parasites. In return for cleaning up fish, the shrimps get a free meal. Cleaner shrimps often sway their bodies as they move, which – together with their bright colours – may help to scare away predators.

COLOURFUL SLUGS

Many sea slugs are brilliant colours to warn predators that they have poisonous skins and will taste terrible. Some sea slugs even steal the stinging cells of corals and sea anemones and use them for their own defence. Another useful trick is to steal some tiny plants from the corals and grow them in their own bodies as an extra food supply.

CORAL COASTS

Coral reefs contain the greatest variety of life of any sea community. The Great Barrier Reef of Australia has over 3,000 different species of animal, and coral reefs in total support one-third of all the world's fish species. The large amount of reef life is because of the constant warmth and light, as well as the great supply of oxygen brought by the waves breaking over the reef. Coral reefs are ancient environments. Having grown on Earth for some 450 million years, they have developed very different plants and animals that all live together. A reef consists of a thin layer of coral animals on top of layer upon layer of empty coral skeletons. Many creatures, from fish, clams and sea lilies to sponges, moray eels and octopuses, feed or make their homes in the branches of the reef. The bright colours of reef fish, may help species to recognise each other in the crowd.

BLENDING IN

The colours and patterns of the hawkfish blend in well with a background of coral. This predator often hides itself in coral for greater camouflage. Then it can dart out to make surprise attacks on the fish it eats. This deep-water hawkfish is generally found on outer reef slopes at depths of 40 metres (131 ft) or more.

REEF BUILDERS

The Great Barrier Reef is the biggest coral reef in the world. It stretches for 2,300 km (1,430 miles) along the north-eastern coast of Australia. At low tide, the reef seems to stretch to the horizon. During very low spring tides, the corals are exposed to the air for some hours. Corals are strange animals. They have a simple body with one opening for food and waste that moves in and out of the body. Most corals live in colonies built up by one founder individual, which then divides itself to grow new versions of itself, over and over again.

YOUNG SEAWEEDS

EDIBLE PERIWINKLE

EDIBLE CRAB

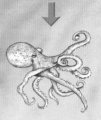

LESSER OCTOPUS

Octopuses are intelligent predators that usually feed at night. They glide over the sea bed until they are within about 20 cm (8 inches) of their prey. Then they pounce, using jets of water to shoot forwards and catch the prey with their sucker-tipped arms. Octopuses have a highly developed sense of touch and can feel into cracks in between rocks to detect crabs and shellfish hiding there.

PREDATORS & PREY

SHORE STINGERS

Anemones cannot move quickly to chase prey but their tentacles wave about in the water to grab tiny floating creatures or larger animals such as fish and prawns. Barbed stings in the tentacles help to subdue the prey and paralyse it. The tentacles pass the prey down to the mouth opening and then spread out again to catch more food.

From razor-sharp teeth, bills and claws, to barbed harpoons, stinging tentacles and super-strong suckers, coastline predators have the right tools to catch their prey. Sea otters even use stones to smash open the tough shells of sea snails or brush off the sharp spines of sea urchins. One hunting strategy is to lie in wait for prey, like an anemone; ambushing prey, like an octopus; or chasing it, like a seal or a cormorant. Shellfish are well protected by their strong shells but even these can be pulled apart by a starfish or drilled through by a dog whelk or an oyster drill. Killer whales are true hunters. They hunt in groups and are able to catch large prey, such as seals. The great baleen whales, such as blue whales and sperm whales filter tiny animals from the water. They are also called predators because they take living prey from their environment.

REEF SHARKS

These Caribbean reef sharks are hunting at the edge of a coral reef. Other reef sharks include the white-tipped and black-tipped reef sharks, tiger sharks and hammerheads. A shark's sharp teeth help it to grip and cut up its prey. When the front teeth wear out, they are replaced by new teeth growing behind them. One shark can get through thousands of teeth in its lifetime.

BOXING SHRIMP

Mantis shrimps hunt for smaller shrimps, crabs and fish. One pair of limbs has evolved to form 'fists' rather like boxing gloves. These suddenly shoot out to deliver an impact like a bullet, to smash or stun their prey.

SPOTTED HUNTER

The leopard seal patrols coastal waters near a penguin colony, waiting for the penguins to dive into the water. It is a speedy seal with a long, flexible neck and a wide mouth for grasping penguins, seal pups and other prey. Leopard seals pursue their prey under the water and then beat them against the surface to loosen the skin. This skin may peel right away from the body and collect up around the neck. Small penguins are usually swallowed whole.

SNAIL DRILLS

Rocky shore snails, such as oyster drills, dog whelks and necklace shells, have to work quite hard for their meals. They pour a softening fluid over the shells of prey, such as mussels, barnacles (left) and limpets, and then drill a hole in the shell using their tongue. A dog whelk may take two days to drill through a limpet or mussel shell, eventually making a very neat, circular hole. Some of these drilling snails have a special tooth on the rim of their shells to help them pull open the shells of clams and mussels.

SEASHORE FOOD CHAIN

PLANT & ANIMAL PLANKTON

PEACOCK FANWORM

FLOUNDER

HERON

Many seashore animals are filter feeders, such as fan worms. They take in large quantities of water and pump it out through a kind of filter, which traps food particles for the animal to eat. Since they often filter both plant and animal plankton from the water, filter-feeders are called omnivores, which means they eat both plants and animals.

DEFENCE

ROCKY BURROW

Piddocks use the teeth along the edge of their shells to drill through rock, turning one way and then the other, just like a drill bit. The piddock depends on its burrow to provide protection and is lives only partly inside its shell. Piddocks cannot detect each other's presence in the rock and one piddock may drill slowly straight through another.

Coastlines are busy, bustling places, full of creatures trying to eat each other. Some creatures, such as fish, octopuses and squid can swim away from danger. Even scallops can close their shells to escape the grip of a starfish. Hiding in burrows or among rocks or coral gives animals that do not move around a better chance of survival. Many are well camouflaged: the decorator crab makes its own camouflage from bits of seaweed and small animals; the weedy sea dragon is a seahorse that looks just like a piece of seaweed. Thick, armour-plated shells protect shellfish against the weather and predators, while hermit crabs cleverly move into an empty shell. More dangerous methods of defence include the sharp spines of sea urchins, the nasty nipping claws of crabs and the poisons of sea slugs. Animals that live in groups, such as fish in shoals or colonies of nesting seabirds, can warn each other of danger and help defend each other.

COAT-OF-MAIL SHELLS

Chitons are sometimes called 'coat-of-mail' shells because their shells are made up of eight overlapping plates joined and surrounded by a stretchy muscle called a girdle. The many plates allow a chiton to bend its body easily and cling tightly to any rock surface. This makes it hard for predators to reach its soft body inside the shell. If a chiton is detached from a surface, it coils up to protect its soft body.

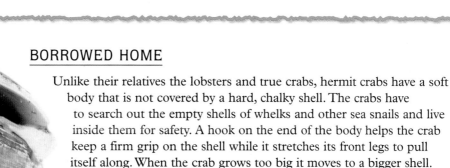

BORROWED HOME

Unlike their relatives the lobsters and true crabs, hermit crabs have a soft body that is not covered by a hard, chalky shell. The crabs have to search out the empty shells of whelks and other sea snails and live inside them for safety. A hook on the end of the body helps the crab keep a firm grip on the shell while it stretches its front legs to pull itself along. When the crab grows too big it moves to a bigger shell.

CRAFTY CAMOUFLAGE

Flatfish are experts in camouflage. Their topsides match the colour of the sea bed so they are almost impossible to see when they keep still. Many flatfish can change their colouring within minutes to match the sea bed. Their underside has no need of special colouring, so it is white or pale in many species.

PRICKLY MOUTHFUL

When puffer fish, or porcupine fish, are threatened, they inflate their bodies with water or air. This makes them too large for most predators to swallow. They also look more frightening. Porcupine fish and some puffer fish are also armed with sharp spines that stick out when they inflate, making them a prickly mouthful.

SPINY PROTECTION

A sea urchin's long spines have three functions: protection, moving about and as digging tools to burrow into rocks. The spines are fixed to the shell of the urchin by muscles around raised areas. This allows them to move in all directions. The spines soon break off when the urchin dies and empty shells are all that is washed up on the beach.

NESTS, EGGS & YOUNG

PREGNANT FATHER

This male seahorse is giving birth to babies which have developed in a pouch on the front of his body. The female lays her eggs in the male's pouch and the young come out after two to seven weeks. As soon as they are born, the young seahorses must look after themselves.

Many animals that live in the oceans, such as penguins, seals and turtles, travel to coastlines in the breeding season because they have to lay their eggs or give birth to their young on land. Warm, shallow coastal waters rich in food are ideal places for young fish to grow up; while nesting on coasts gives seabirds easy access to their food supply. Seabirds and seals feed and take care of their young, but many shore creatures leave their young to look after themselves. They lay a lot of eggs because many will not survive to become adults. Female hermit crabs and some shrimps and some crabs lay fewer eggs but carry them around. The common octopus even guards her eggs in her underground home for about six weeks. The larvae of many invertebrate animals, such as hermit crabs, barnacles and peacock worms, may drift off with the plankton before settling down.

As they grow, invertebrates with external skeletons, such as crabs, have to moult several times.

SEAL PUPS

The common, or harbour, seal gives birth to a single pup in late June or July, usually on sandbars, ledges, offshore islands or ice floes and sometimes in the water. The pup is born well developed and quite independent. It has an adult type of coat, unlike grey seals which have a white coat when they are born. The pups grow fast as they feed on their mother's rich milk.

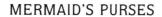

MERMAID'S PURSES

Baby dogfish, which are a small kind of shark, develop inside an egg case called a mermaid's purse. At first the egg case is soft, but it soon hardens in the seawater. Tendrils, which are root-like threads, attach the egg case to seaweed to stop it being swept away by the waves and currents. A large yolk sac inside the egg case feeds the dogfish embryo for up to ten months before it hatches out to start a life of its own.

CORAL SNOWSTORM

Corals release masses of eggs and sperm into the water, usually just after a full moon in spring or early summer. Some people have described the coral spawning as 'an upside-down snowstorm'. If a sperm fertilises an egg from the same coral species, a tiny swimming larva develops. This drifts with the plankton before settling down to develop into an adult. Some coral eggs are fertilised while still on the adult, then looked after and released over time. Corals can also reproduce by dividing into two again and again to produce exact copies of themselves.

BREEDING MIGRATION

Small fish called grunions migrate in breeding shoals of many thousands to the sandy shores of Californian coasts during the high spring tides. The females wriggle through the wet sand and lay their eggs, which are then fertilised by the male. Two weeks later, when the tides are again very high, the young fish hatch. They squirm through the sand and into the sea.

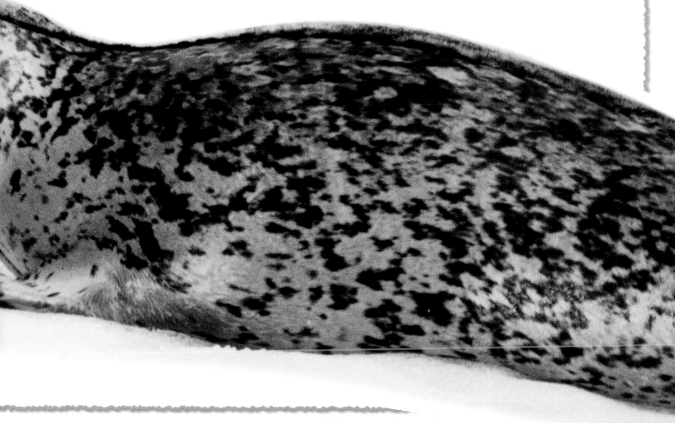

PEOPLE & COASTLINES

DIVING

The underwater environment is alien to us and can only be truly experienced through diving. Aqualungs, developed in the early 1940s by Jacques Cousteau and Emile Gagnan, have changed the way we explore coastal waters, both for fun and scientific research. This diver is freeing a spiny lobster caught among the fronds of a giant seaweed called kelp. Coral reefs can be damaged by heavy boat anchors and by divers hunting for souvenirs.

For thousands of years, people have lived by the sea so they can fish and earn a living. Today, 60 per cent of the world's population lives on, or near, the coast. Many of the world's major cities, such as New York, San Francisco, Sydney or Shanghai are located on coasts where there are natural harbours, or where rivers meet the sea. This is useful for transporting goods carried by sea to other towns and cities. Mining can also be carried out in shallow coastal waters, such as dredging for tin in Thailand or mining diamonds off the Namibian coast. Drilling for oil and gas may occur off the coast. In some countries, farmland has been reclaimed from the sea or from coastal marshlands and shellfish or pearl oysters are farmed near the shore. Coastlines the world over are also important places for tourism and leisure activities.

TOURIST JAM

On this crowded beach in Malia, Crete, there is hardly any space for the people, let alone wildlife. Birds and turtles that nest on beaches are often disturbed by the noise and bright lights in tourist areas. Beaches that are especially important for wildlife can be protected and new tourist developments can be planned to avoid areas of special value to wildlife.

FISHING COMMUNITIES

Colourful houses and fishing boats are a familiar sight on the coasts of the Caribbean islands, where fishing is a way of life for many. Around the world, small fishing communities are important to a coastal region as they supply food and act as a place of trade.

BEACH POLLUTION

Shorelines are narrow strips of land that can often become covered with rubbish left by people or washed up by the tides. Animals can injure themselves or become ill if they eat it. This fragile environment is full of life but can easily be damaged by the things we throw away.

FOOD FROM THE SEA

Many people who live near the sea work in the fishing industry or harvest other seafood, such as shellfish or octopuses. To make sure of a regular supply of oysters, this oyster farmer grows them in special cages in shallow waters. The oysters grow best in clean water.

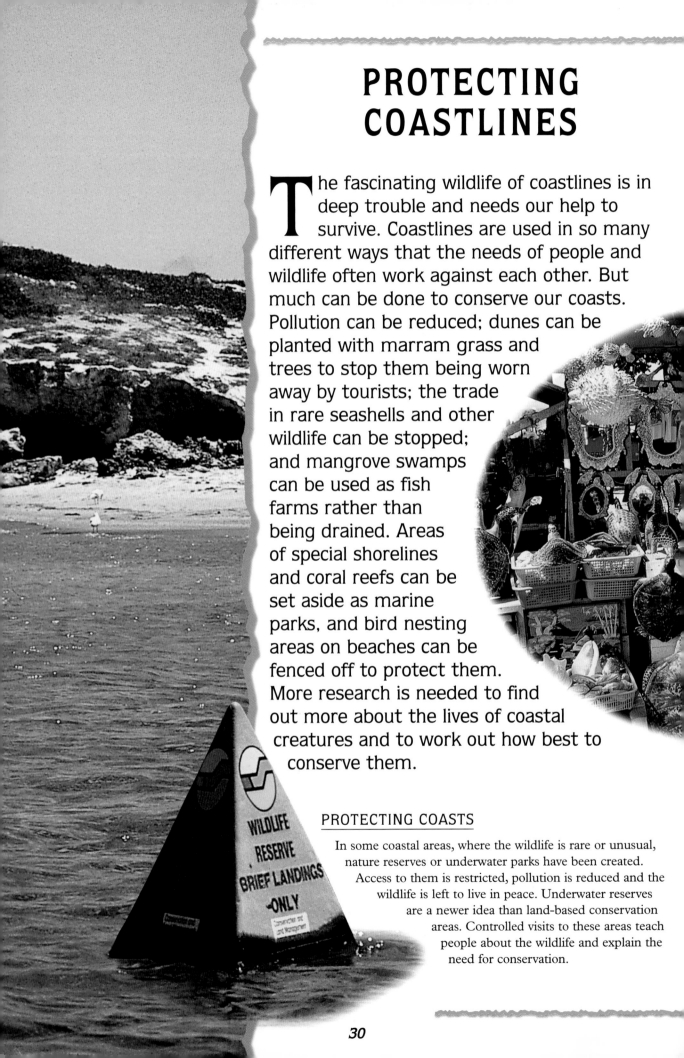

PROTECTING COASTLINES

The fascinating wildlife of coastlines is in deep trouble and needs our help to survive. Coastlines are used in so many different ways that the needs of people and wildlife often work against each other. But much can be done to conserve our coasts. Pollution can be reduced; dunes can be planted with marram grass and trees to stop them being worn away by tourists; the trade in rare seashells and other wildlife can be stopped; and mangrove swamps can be used as fish farms rather than being drained. Areas of special shorelines and coral reefs can be set aside as marine parks, and bird nesting areas on beaches can be fenced off to protect them. More research is needed to find out more about the lives of coastal creatures and to work out how best to conserve them.

PROTECTING COASTS

In some coastal areas, where the wildlife is rare or unusual, nature reserves or underwater parks have been created. Access to them is restricted, pollution is reduced and the wildlife is left to live in peace. Underwater reserves are a newer idea than land-based conservation areas. Controlled visits to these areas teach people about the wildlife and explain the need for conservation.

RESEARCH

This manx shearwater has been caught at night so it can be tagged and its movements traced. These little birds come to land only to breed and spend the winter feeding at sea. Tagging these shearwaters has shown that they migrate from Britain to South America every year, flying at least 740 km (460 miles) a day. It takes them 16 days or so to make this extraordinary journey. The more we know about coastal wildlife, the better we will be able to take care of it.

TRADE WARS

This souvenir stall in Java is selling the shells of endangered turtles. If all tourists refused to buy such souvenirs, fewer rare animals would be taken from the wild. It is not always easy to recognise the rare species so it is best to buy souvenirs made by people.

COASTAL DEFENCES

Coastlines are always changing shape as the waves and weather erode the rocks. Some coasts are being worn away while others are being built up as loose material is washed up to form new and larger beaches. People often try to protect coasts by building concrete or rocky defences. But the sea is a powerful force and in the long term there is little we can do. In the future, many coastlines will be affected by problems, such as rising sea levels caused by global warming.

STRANDED WHALE

Whales may die at sea and be washed up on the shore but live whales sometimes swim onto the beach and strand themselves. Why they do this is still a mystery but it may have something to do with illness, pollution or problems with the whales' navigation system. People sometimes save stranded whales by keeping them covered with water and helping them swim back out to sea when the tide comes in. Watching live whales off the coast is a growing tourist industry in many countries.

GLOSSARY

Adaptation A change in an animal or plant that makes it better suited to the environment it lives in.

Dredging Digging out and gathering material from the sea bottom.

Estuary A place where freshwater rivers and streams flow into the ocean, mixing with the seawater.

Fossil The remains of a creature or plant from millions of years ago, the imprint of which is preserved in rock.

Fronds The leaf-like parts of seaweed that grow out in branches and are used for photosynthesis.

Global warming The increase in the Earth's temperature, caused in part by the Greenhouse Effect – a build up of gases in the atmosphere.

Invertebrate An animal that does not have a backbone, such as an ant.

Omnivore A kind of animal that eats both plants and animals, rather than just favouring one of them.

Photosynthesis The process used by plants to make food from light energy, carbon dioxide and water.

Spawning When a fish deposits large quantities of eggs into the ocean.

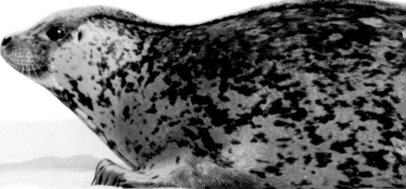

ACKNOWLEDGEMENTS

We would like to thank: Helen Wire and Elizabeth Wiggans for their assistance. Artwork by Peter Bull Art Studio.

Copyright © 2009 *ticktock* Entertainment Ltd

First published in Great Britain by *ticktock* Media Ltd, The Old Sawmill, 103 Goods Station Road, Tunbridge Wells, Kent TN1 2DP, Great Britain

All rights reserved. No part of this publication may be reproduced, stored in a retrieval system, or transmitted in any form or by any means electronic, mechanical, photocopying, recording or otherwise, without prior written permission of the copyright owner.

A CIP catalogue record for this book is available from the British Library.

ISBN 978 1 84898 000 6 (paperback)

ISBN 978 1 84898 045 7 (hardback)

Picture research by Image Select. Printed in China.

Picture Credits: t=top, b=bottom, c=centre, l=left, r=right, OFC=outside front cover, OBC=outside back cover, IFC=inside front cover

Biofotos; 20/21b, 24/25b, 25br, 26/27t, 30/31c. Heather Angel; 2/3b, 3cr, 3tr, 4tl, 4bl, 4br, 5cr, 8br, 8bl, 9tl, 10/11(main), 12br, 12/13t, 13br, 14/15c, 15tr, 16bl, 16/17t, 18l, 18t, 19tl, 19tr, 23bl, 24tl, 31cr. Oxford Scientific Films; 9tr, 11bl, 11tr, 13c, 13tr, 14/15b, 16tl, 17ct, 19c, 23cr, 24bl, 26tl, 27tr, 27cr, 30l, 31t. Shutterstock; OFC. Tony Stone; IFC, 2/3t, 2l, 2ct, 4/5(main), 6l, 6/7b, 6/7t, 7tr, 7br, 10tl, 11cr, 12bl, 14l, 15bl, 14t, 16/17mp, 18/19b, 20tl, 21r, 21ct, 20cr, 22/23t, 22tl, 22bl, 25cr, 24/25t, 26/27b & 32, 28l, 28/29c, 28ct, 29tr, 29cr, 31br OBC (both).

Every effort has been made to trace the copyright holders and we apologise in advance for any unintentional omissions. We would be pleased to insert the appropriate acknowledgement in any subsequent edition of this publication.